BACKTALK

T0273331

Also by Robin Becker
Discretion in Personal Effects

Backtalk

poems by
Robin Becker

Grateful acknowledgement is made to the editors of
the following magazines and anthologies in which some
of these poems originally appeared:
*Aspect, The Carolina Quarterly, Dark Horse,
Earth's Daughters, Grist, The Painted Bride Quarterly,
Panache, Princeton Spectrum, The Real Paper, Sojourner,
The Aspect Anthology* (Zephyr Press), *Ourselves and
Our Children* (Random House), *Poets on Photography*
(Dog Ear Press), *Rapunzel, Rapunzel* (McBooks Press)

Thanks to Cummington Community of the Arts,
The Ragdale Foundation, and The Helene Wurlizter
Foundation of New Mexico, where a number of these poems
were written and to the Humanities Department of the
Massachusetts Institute of Technology for its support.

Book design by Mary Rothenbuehler
Cover etching by Jane Kogan
Photograph by Wendy Gross
Typeset by Ed Hogan/Aspect Composition and
pasted-up with the assistance of Melanie Morris
Special thanks to Leslie Lawrence

*Publication of this book was assisted by a grant from the
Massachusetts Council on the Arts & Humanities,
a state agency whose funds are recommended by the Governor
and appropriated by the State Legislature.*

for my grandmother
my parents
and Miriam

CONTENTS

I

II

III

IV

I

NORTH

We can't stop going north, you say,
which means the apples have frozen in the back
and the conniving raven is throwing snow in our faces.
Though we take the first exit and circle,
we're back on the highway heading north.
Like pioneers pressing north by northwest
across the country, like anything Norwegian,
we're getting colder. North, when we want Boston,
safety, meals cooked, households.
Out here, whole neighborhoods float
in the polar waters, and whales turn up
on the village beaches; they are the dead
loosed from circumstance, come back to tell the truth.
At the potlatch, we'll turn our palms up
to the Northern Lights and surrender everything—
we who had so carefully planned and packed,
leaving only the distant future to chance.
When we skid, you clutch my neck and the car swerves,
severing us from the neat chain of drivers.
At the guard rail, we stop, confounded by time and direction.
Silverware, placemats, coffee pots, dishes lie scattered
on the seats; our hearts beat on, we push north.

A LONG DISTANCE

You disappeared through a tunnel in July;
that was Logan in Boston, my city, a day
when the airport was bright with arrivals.
I lost my imagination,
couldn't picture you once you were gone.
7th grade was a large empty map
with the continents drawn in.
I remember Africa:
Se-ne-gal, Gui-nea, Si-er-ra Le-one,
Li-be-ri-a, I-vo-ry Coast.
The rhythms of the words held the countries
& the curve of north Africa in place.
The New York Times says
there is a national strike in your country;
by the time I get an overseas operator,
you're recovering from amoebic dysentery.
I hear my voice clacking over the lines,
& I remember the globe that was a pencil sharpener.
I remember standing in the lunchroom
& trying to figure out
how I could be standing in the lunchroom
& standing on the earth which was the globe.
One night I dream the globe is flattened.
You start climbing north—up to me.
The dream ends with you in Tunisia—
a tiny figure climbing—
until the globe is folded in half.

A GOOD EDUCATION

First, there's daddy, big spender, picking up
the check & mother glancing into his fist
trying to see. She notices the tags
hanging from the dresses, but in the men's
store, he says *one of these & two of those*
without looking.
                    It wasn't fair, who got
what & why. I never knew what anything cost
until it was *too much* or *cheaply made* or *not for us.*
Fractions I never got either, subtracting pieces
from pieces of things. When it was pies, OK,
but when it was point zero zero four,
I ended up weeping.
                    Geometry was the last straw;
they let me out & shipped me up to Latin—
matching the subject with the verb ending,
searching for the missing preposition.
Latin was like long division: once you memorized
the tables, you kept dividing & dividing until
the row was done. On & on the numbers fell
like a connect-the-dots game. As long as you knew
the multiplication tables, the numbers
came out perfectly divided.
                    Next came word problems,
questions of ladders & shadows & the sides of houses.
How did you get the little phrase right up next
to the word it modified, so that you didn't have
the farmhouse marching through the grass but the farmer?
You had to scoot the unnecessary parts up close
to the necessary man sweating through the fields.
                    Every week,
there were at least six new things every day.
Who could keep up? Laura & Anne & Penny Sharp
were neck and neck; I was the class clown, in the middle,

thank God not at the bottom like Betsy & Suzanne.
The periods were fifty minutes; if it was your good subject,
you wanted it to last; if it was your bad, you tried,
you tried to understand what she was writing on the board,
but you were wishing that someone would throw up,
or there would be a fire drill, or like the day when
     Kennedy died,
everyone had to go home with her mother.

WOMEN IN LOVE

The horses you rode when you were a child
come bucking and rearing into my afternoon.
You're hanging on, a skinny kid,
clutching some mane in a frieze that winds
like a bandage around my room, where a fence
supports a man violent in his watching.
He is my father, your father, fathers
wanting to promise everything.
He walks to the drug store, goes to a show,
keeps an appointment downtown.

Someday I might wander the streets
of Provincetown
like a woman I used to watch—
all her possessions in a shopping bag—
sitting in a pizza joint in the center of town.
She ate a slice slowly
talking to herself
and wiping her endless fingers.
Once, alone on the beach midday,
I saw her sitting under a pier,
her life curled up beside her
in a canvas bag.

We stand before the day lilies—
bright petals reflexed
and several swords about to burst.
I think of O'Keeffe's great flowers,
stubbornly themselves and not themselves.
You say *I don't know what I used to think
about women in love with each other;
that it was distorted, something blown
out of proportion.*

You walk through the meadow
looking for a way
out of anger and desire.
We disturb the difficult compromises
with our steady wanting of each other,
but for a moment the afternoon light
falls on your shoulder, our intimacy is loosed
into the air, and you move easily
down the path, parting the prairie grass.

FAMILY ALBUM

Mother runs across the yard,
a blur of summer cotton.
She does not see my sister slipping
on the sidewalk outside the frame.
This she will not see for years
while pictures accrue in the albums
& I dress up like Peter Pan
& my sister falls from her bike
& we wave *bye-bye* in the Poconos.

And the cousins grow big & get married
& I resemble strange creatures
for which my parents have no names.
Mother, you always loved that photo,
the one where I was an Indian brave.
We reappear as young ladies
out for dinner with the family.
The awkward years, my mother explains.
Abruptly, the album ends.

Will the lovely eleven-year-old
come to ruin? Will the child astride
the pony ever get over her fear?
Who can find the one
who will grow up to be the painter?
In this family, everyone looks normal:
daddy holds baby on the beach; sisters pose
in the yard; cousins gather for a birthday party.
But where is the tomboy careening down the street,
carrying branches for camouflage?
Where is the Indian with leaves in her pockets?

STUDIES FROM LIFE

You dove in the wake of a lobster boat.
From the rocks I watched women
bending for shells; you swam, kids played,
men hauled silver buckets up the beach.
If love is seeing, I loved seeing you
cutting the water with your thin arms.

*   *   *

Hands deep in the raspberry bushes,
we stood talking with our backs to each other.

*   *   *

You cross the room, slice a pineapple; the juice
runs down your fingers. Late afternoon.
This is a scene I might analyze
the way I would a dream: a woman in amber
pours cream; I am the woman and I am the person
for whom the cream is poured.
        Window. Wooden board. Pitcher.
The simple arrangement of objects.

*   *   *

We sit at the table. If love is seeing,
I saw the pale room lit by candles,
your wrist and the darkness behind.
It held you, I saw it, now is it mine?

IN CONVERSATION

When your name comes up
in conversation over dinner,
I come to your defense.
She looked beautiful, someone said,
*but unsettled. She left a suitcase
in the shed.* As if you left me here
to cover—an extra ear, hand, eye—
or to mount your reputation.
I know what I know from experience:
you were a strong swimmer;
you defected from your family;
you made love like a person
who had to catch a plane.
By the end of the meal, you're larger
than life, an outlaw with class.
When we gather before the fire,
couples lie in each other's arms,
those alone climb into themselves.
Like a diligent agent
stationed in a foreign country,
I'm waiting for a signal
to come home.

THE CHINESE LUNAR CALENDAR HOROSCOPE

You were born in the Year of the Dragon which accounts for your stubbornness, the way you say *no* over & over when we're talking long distance. People born in the Year of the Dragon should settle down with those born in the Year of the Monkey. These people also talk too much but are extremely loyal. Loyalty will come in handy, as dragons do not listen to advice & like to break away when they have a chance. People born in the Year of the Dragon are healthy & fit which does not explain your nine colds this year, not to mention flu & hypochondria.

I was born in the Year of the Rabbit & will probably succeed in business as rabbits inspire confidence & are fortunate in money matters. These qualities explain why I always have a job & can pay the plane fare, while you, ambitious but lacking foresight, miss the plane & depend upon your friends the serpents who always help others, even those who are beautiful. People born in the Year of the Rabbit should take up with those born in the Year of the Boar. Boar-people are industrious & honest if a little dull, which would be a relief after all this travelling.

BERKSHIRE COUNTY JOURNAL

Sliding   backwards in second
power slips   from my hands
rocking   in a deathcar
on a highway   of ice

Minarets
of pine & spruce   rise
against the mountains   winter light

2

I nail the windows shut
& bolt the skylight
Still I dream   the studio blows apart
Logs smoulder   All night
mice run in the walls
wind blasts the cabin

3

The January sky
deepens
Stars shoot
a chemical language
illuminate a secret code
The Big Dipper   grows bigger
pitching forward

4

I stop to look at cows
the farm a picturebook
red barn   silo   tractor   hay
The animals   fixed in their snowy field
rotate their heads

Sunset   a flare of pink
in a cow's nostril
Behind   the fairgrounds sink
silent   deeper
like a wedge   each empty barn leans
into the snow

5

In a dream   I meet a woman I loved
She says   *I'm spinning*
like another kind of energy
We talk   as if she is here
a force   I must contend with
like fire or cold

WHEN FRIENDS LEAVE

for Brad Crenshaw and Debra Gorlin

Breakfast is no fun
                    Boots are silent
No one bangs his head   No one falls
                        laughing in the snow
When friends leave   snow flies horizontal
The dog cries at the door
                    every chair is irritable
The wooden bowl waits upside down
                    coats are hung on hooks in the hall
We do not talk about the oak pegs
                    and the house of hewn logs
Brad does not pretend to be the itinerant thatcher
                    come to mend the roof
And we wish   stopping to have a few words with the farmer
that he was here to see the cows hunker against the barn
We sit close   near the stove   feel their shadows
pass behind us reaching for books   We do not pretend
            to live in Holland
                    under the same roof
            with animals and fodder
When they were here   we found shingles of elm bark
trails through birch meadows   a silo with a cupola
Now we remember the patient eyes of Debra   beautiful
            listening   and the happy arrangement
of stones in their courses   lacing a path through the field

ON NOT BEING ABLE TO IMAGINE THE FUTURE

Picture the house,
the furniture, the cat,
or you may never have them.
In order to possess
you must envision.
If you fail to imagine your lover
you won't recognize her on the street
when opportunity presents itself
like a bill in the grass.
If you're nearing thirty
practice feeling forty or fifty.
If you don't train
you'll never learn
to play the violin or grow old.
Time will pass
but you won't be able to retire
or plan ahead
because you never planned ahead.
There will be no summer house,
no lake in New Hampshire,
no packing up the car,
no beautiful small children.
A trunk slams,
everyone piles in,
this is someone else's life.

QUABBIN RESERVOIR

We inherited
a condemned town,
sealed
like a Mason jar
before I was born.
When I was seven
I packed my things,
sat in Howe's Store,
watched them take the Vegetable Pills
and Essential Oils
from the shelves.
Years later, I returned
with my sisters and brother.
Like tourists, we rowed
across the Reservoir,
the memory of solid ground
like a theorem
that could not be proved.

2
I used to dream
of flying
on Noah's great ark;
a winged ship
would transport us
to a mirror of the Valley
where we tethered ourselves
to the earth
like flagpoles
driven deep.

3

My grandma owned a dry goods store in Enfield where she
sketched the buildings in the Valley: Blacksmith, Harness,
Grange Hall, Stone Mill. She read the newspapers aloud; I
was just a little girl, but I knew she was keeping records of
the town we'd never see again. My mother made men's suits
and wrote letters to Boston. *A thousand acres must not be
flooded. We will not leave our homes or disinter our dead.*
My grandma died, we moved to Vermont, someone gave me
her book of buildings.

4

Now my sisters walk
onto the slippery
assemblage of rocks.
We talk
about sleigh-riding
with freestones
to warm our feet,
grandma's sketchbook
wedged between us.
I remember the names
of the towns—
Dana, Prescott, Millington—
and try to trace the shoreline,
accounting for each stone,
wondering like the surveyor
what constitutes water
what constitutes land.

VERMONT/JANUARY

Snow falls on the planks   between the cracks
black and white stripes   snow; no snow; snow
Inside we practice silence   like members
of a religious order   we keep our promises

to each other

pass from room to room
stare out of windows
Years ago   I shared a cabin by the sea
with a painter   She said   *The cabin seems to grow larger*
                  when we're quiet   It's as if
                  the walls expand and breathe

             *   *   *

Someone has readied her house for us: a key   wood by the stove
candles   extra blankets   We slip in and begin to unpack
Our things tell our stories   The dog claims a place
but I'm shy; someone has readied a house
with a view of the mountains   and I feel unworthy
                  The beams are three feet wide
                  There is a beautiful table   carved chairs
I want to cry when I touch the wood
                  So many windows
                  O when we lie in bed we see the sky

             *   *   *

I practice not hearing you   until I do not hear you
turning pages, walking, picking up wood

My eyes follow the drifts to the snowfence
defending the road   Snow thickens on the planks
fills the cracks   makes an irregular design

You rise to check the stove   your arm pale
against the cast iron   This is our second year

and I practice
coming back to this desk, this place, here.

*   *   *

I used to think there would be time   for everything:
houses, horses, the study of many languages,
honing my body to its most honest self

Today, running up the hill behind you,
it was like this: no one else on the road   distant dogs barking
a farmhouse   You reached the crest and disappeared

I heard my own blood and turned—
                    the valley snow-covered   the violet trees
                    ridges giving way to ridges   the lines
                    like the lines in your hand

THE SKETCHBOOK

for Kate

The sketchbook tells the story of the journey:
hours sitting in the heat and dust;
how you endured direct sun, midday light in Arizona—
the church closed for repairs, the museum crowded.

Thin brush strokes show #4 on the Beaufort Wind Scale
raises dust and loose paper; you were caught in #6
when the paintbox overturned. Telephone wires whistled,
a smattering of dots covered the record.

Turn the page, we're holding steady, magnetic north,
into the mountains vivid and fresh.
A stream of purple: moccasin flower, violet.
For the mesas, a slash of ochre and emerald green.

The sketches find you dreaming of home,
writing in the names of the colors
instead of mixing paint. The grass is humming
words you've never used: *pampas, sagebrush, alkaline.*

When the highway veers left, we follow,
plunge into a canyon where you might have waited
days for a good mechanic. Sketch after sketch
of roadside: cactus, piñon, a hawk's scalloped wing.

PHONE CALL AT 1 AM

You're still giving me the same line about how in ten years,
you'll be one of the best painters in New York City. For a
year you've told me that your kitchen's almost finished. Mean-
while, you eat at the corner, at work, at the place across the
street. You've ruined another painting. You say you didn't
know when to stop. I think of all the poems that die, turn
hard & brittle once the effort is over. You hate to admit
anything's over. That summer, I lost my watch, & you be-
lieved it would turn up. When you left your glasses at the
river, I laughed. Now, you explain why you haven't written,
what snagged you in my letter. I imagine you reading, ready
with a pencil to argue in the margins. Track lights remind me
of you & the smell of turpentine; black turtlenecks & haircuts
that end in perfect triangles, as if the shape would last forever.

LETTERS TO MICHAEL

She had a penchant for the stories of strangers and young boys. Once, after a trip to New York by train, she told me about a fourteen-year-old who accompanied her as far as Stamford. He studied ballet and early American film. They sat in the dining car, drank ginger ale, and looked through the big ballet book he carried.

When the train pulled into Stamford, she watched him greet his family. She was struck by his father—youngish, athletic, wearing a pullover and jeans. When the boy saw him, he rushed forward, dropped his bags, and they embraced.

2

We were like kids that summer, running around the countryside, in love with the landscape and each other. We wrestled after breakfast and went painting in the woods. We carried canvas chairs and brushes, we held out our fingers and squinted to gauge perspective.

Later, when I came to write my own story of the summer, I discovered that my vocabulary had changed; my rhythms were different.

3

Michael, there is more to the story; I tell it to you in pieces, the way I think of it now. Mornings in the large dining hall, I'd see her at a distance, scowling, detached, angry. She knew I'd been with you the night before. When she rose to get coffee, I'd take my cup and meet her at the coffee pot for a moment.

She was always watching us, you and me, as we came
and went. She knew when you were in New York, when I
was off with friends in Stockbridge, when we fought, how
the fights ended. In a way, she was the chronicler of our last
months—watching, watching, with a determination I'd never
seen. She was desperate to feel pain. What else could it
have been? Sometimes, walking down to your cabin, I'd
turn and find her staring at me from a window in the barn.

Once I stole into her studio. I knew she wouldn't
return until dinner, so I smoked her cigarettes and read her
journal. It was filled with descriptions of the places we'd
visited—lovely, detailed studies of the woods and back roads.
And it was filled with our conversations, dialogues repro-
duced verbatim with an accuracy that stunned me. What
was she recording, and why? There were little plays, too,
in which she argued for you, explaining my ambivalence,
my fear of losing you Michael, my gestures, my words.

SUCH AN ALLIANCE

she fears
would not be possible
with a man
so much younger
Though they meet
in the office cafeteria
every day for lunch
& study topographic maps
& natural history
Though he made her a map
of covered bridges
in southern New Hampshire

They meet
in the office cafeteria
for lunch & talk
about the trees & woods
behind the plant
They skate on frozen rivers
at noon   He takes her hand
Still she thinks
he's too young
wouldn't understand what it's like
to be forty & feeling
always like somebody's mother

GREAT EXPECTATIONS

All the vegetarians in Cambridge
will end up in your kitchen helping themselves.
I'll be moving down a moving staircase
at the airport, my eyes bounce looking for yours.
You'll be telling me that we
shouldn't pressure ourselves to have a good time

or make love but be true to the truth
like the white-clothed and religious people
in The Conscious Cookery who smile and
know you by name. We'll look at each other
over brown rice and broccoli while the tape
of Buddhist chanting, the one we exercise by,

plays overhead like Chagall & violins & flying cows.
Later your bed will be a train in a French movie.

On the way to Harvard Square, we will stop
for natural candy, not chocolate but carob.
After two, you'll feel sick, wish I'd stopped you.
I will glance inside a bookshop, watch a man
watch you walk by.

You will want to walk by the river where
the fence is down & the ice is melting
& all the marriageable men in Cambridge
bring their big dogs for a run.

WINTER IN LINCOLN PARK CONSERVATORY

Inside the greenhouse
old men on benches
unbutton winter coats
beneath giant fronds.
Pink hands pink necks
they thrive
like tropical birds
in a swirl
of compound leaves.
From the glass dome
radiate generations—
vines shining green
arms & legs entwined.

One gentleman
takes my hand.
We examine
columbian palms
banana trees
orchids.
I think of sex
& the fact
that there is no
dormant season
in a hothouse.
The plantains
advance
against the panes
immense oblong sheaths.

The old man
excuses himself
through the glass.
He vanishes
behind azalea
blooming red white pink
flourishing flourishing
unnaturally
in the steamy air.

ON BEING LITERAL-MINDED

There are no fish in the air
& the lawn chairs are nothing
but chairs though they remind you
of dolphins & old men on stretchers.
And the black horses in your dreams
are not mythic,
neither your childish totems
nor your own dogs transformed,
just a piece of daily life—
the gelding cantering figure eights
in Duxbury or Degas' racers
off postcards you meant to send
from the museum in Boston.
Your old lover who knows
it's over will not reconsider
though you write her into stories
doing things she'd never do in life.
In life, she's sweaty, walking to town,
too depressed to work, too distracted
to read & you're stuck with the facts
this hot June morning, hearing the birds
for what they are, wondering
what to do with the horse
who reappears each night
& shrinks down into the shape
of the puppy by morning.

GHAZAL: THE IMPASSE

Sun glints on a metal box of watercolor paints.
Wind stills to a silence like emergency.

We sit in parallel lines, birds on a telephone wire.
Light changes from second to second.

She says it's possible to love more than one person.
Wearing clothes I've given her, she stands to buy a ticket.

Aspens shudder on a summer evening.
I take my paints into the woods.

The room smells of linseed oil and turpentine.
Two paintings face each other like lovers holding their ground.

OLD WOMEN AND HILLS

The road to Chimayo
winds
up the mountain
& down
to the fleshy foothills.
They open, pink, like the folds
of skin—
clean, loose, soft—
on my grandmother's
upper arm & belly.
Bubbie, I see you
everywhere in the unfamiliar
landscape.
At Santa Ana Pueblo, three old women
introduce the corn dance.
They shuffle across the plaza,
breasts drooping in black
dresses, chanting in Tewa
a monotonous
drone
like the ones
I heard you chant
over candles
when I was a child.
When they raised their arms,
I bowed my head,
seeing you,
black-veiled,
above me.

SIDESHOW

It was January,
it was five-fifteen.
I could read the numbers
on the digital watch
I gave you on your birthday.
We were still in that other
kind of time; I could tell
from the way you cocked your head
and because your lips were slightly parted
and your eyes glazed over.
My body hadn't learned
how desire slips away,
how the familiar starts to grate,
and love turns to a passion
for travel, houses,
a few intense moments
between strangers,
to vanity, to memory.

You had another kind of vanity:
the charge of light
by whose grace
the ordinary was allowed,
speech was permitted,
work was advanced.
In every memory of that time
within time,
I break with it, from it,
out into the world
which hounded us
with civic matters—
where love was a sideshow—
but we—freakish,

dumbstruck—helped ourselves
like gluttons to more
and then like patients
on Stelazine
came the long way back.

CREATIVE WRITING

Please show the highway—desolate—
& the local people. I'd like to feel
something for your characters
but here you're telling, telling, telling
instead of giving one clear image.
What do you mean by *depressing*?
Can you give me an example?
Please come to conference.
Perhaps we can work this out together.
Bring a photo of the pueblo
& the mountains & the fog . . .
I know you saw what you saw
but your job is to prove it:
to show us how you walked
in that particular dirt on that particular day,
stepping from the cool adobe into the light
with no words for anything,
six hundred feet above the muddy Rio Grande.

AFTER MAKING LOVE

Afterwards I like to talk about it,
hear her describe the camels
parading one by one across the desert,
compare notes, find out how the experimental
parts worked. Though it's embarrassing,
I even like to tell her what I see:
supermarkets, shoppers, the students
milling around outside my office,
the cigarette I'll have when it's over.
She finds this curious, worse,
a waste of good time
when she could be
sleeping or going to the bathroom.
And she finds me wordy.
Go to sleep, she says &
turns over. It's OK.
More than once I've lain
stretched out alone smoking
while some pragmatist
wanting a little peace
went to bed. Someday
I'll run into a good talker,
somebody willing to stay up
for hours
visual & verbose.

PRAIRIE

We break off weeds
and put them in each other's mouths.
She slides her fingers
up the milkweed's stem, slits the pod
to watch the seeds float
in the fog beside me.
She pulls me down.
It's the way I thought it would be
when I was seventeen.
The ground is wet. I bury my head
in her chest. She rubs her cheek
against mine—the laws of heat and energy
proven in our bodies.
Here, the illusion of safety—
this is all that matters.
Two women in a field
in the middle of our lives,
while the whole wrecked world
slides into tomorrow.
Her hands come to my body and I would rest
in that simplicity. This field this night
is where we kiss
over and over, clothed, tense.
Before we walk back, she's already walked back,
arranged herself into the familiar fictions.
I remember how she stood among the tourists
the day I thought she wouldn't show,
and we went walking through the galleries
naming the places we'd go: *Etretat,*
Argenteuil, Giverny.

ILLINOIS WINTER

Behind the house the prairie stretches
blue shadows on frozen snow.
We walk bundled like kids in snowsuits
over a stone bridge
past meadows of goldcnrod & aster
encased in ice.
You name the trees & show me
the berries of a hawthorn.
In May, seventy-two kinds of wildflowers
will grow on this prairie
where today our breath rises
like smoke.
Something about the land, you say,
your words lost in the wind.
Inside, the firewood's so dry
the flames rise in seconds,
the sun burns yellow & drops
behind the trees. For a moment,
the room is a bonfire of light—
your glass of scotch a small blaze.

DOCUMENTARY

You say it doesn't have to be
so cut & dried like day or night,
friends or lovers. You say this
for two years
in every major eastern city
while numerous house guests sleep
in the dark behind you.
Life is long, you remind me
long distance, while I edit films
reeling like a Love Documentary:
nights I watched you
watch every man who came into the bar
& later every woman; your body
never quite filling your clothes—
pants baggy, shirt blowing.
You say you're in my life
for keeps like blood sisters,
that I can count on you.
Splice: a dog sleeps in the sun,
columbine grows behind a shed,
a door swings open
& you walk towards me—
your arms outstretched, your face
a shock of summer light.

MAPLE SUGARING

a Currier and Ives print, 1872

Sap in a cauldron and a man
in a red jerkin   others in black
Secondary cauldrons burn in the background
Neighbors come down the path
between the stumps

His wife and daughter in the doorway
of the secondary house
Smoke from the chimney   smoke
from the cauldrons

        This man in his red jerkin
        his pleasure   his wood
        his blue snow   his nightmare of the sled
        his sled   his hill   his sugarbush

        ungloved hands   five evergreens

simple smoke
simple man
in the foreground of his family
with his acres   his nightmares

        his hours   his hours   This morning
        he stands in the sugarbush   this man
        with his terrible dream close in 1872
        close as the bearded chins of his nephews

His sap will spoil
his clear vision will blur   disaster
holds us   to what matters
his cabin will burn
his children will rebel   his neighbors will hate him

THE IMMIGRANT'S STORY

for Laura Weiner

A child walks
into the village
with a cow.
A woman sells
fabric from a wagon.
Uniformed and gleaming
the Czar's men fill the streets.
Everything that follows
is the immigrant's story:
at fifteen she's in Bremen,
tickets in hand for New York.
Later she's vomiting aboard ship.
When her brother
meets her at the station,
she holds out his photograph—
black coat, long beard.

From the factories,
the brick row houses,
she walks to the kosher hotels
where everyone knows the old songs.
The immigrant's story
ends in New Jersey,
grandchildren grown,
friends gone.

In her schoolyard dream,
children flip baseball cards against a wall.
Boys play tag, cement shreds their knees.
This spring the children wear cotton jackets
with zippers flopping silver charms.
A girl stands off to the side.
She feels for the cloth

against her thighs, for the blouse
covering her shoulders.
There is none!
If only she can make it
to the brick school warm as a cow,
she will gather her shame in one place,
knock softly for help,
hold out a picture,
ask for work at the clothing factory
in the only language she knows.

HOCKEY SEASON

Maples, willows, sycamores hid the field
behind the Lower School & meeting house.
We ran in light blue tunics billowing
like maternity tops, cloth sashes looped
round our necks. Elastic from the bloomers
left little marks circling our thighs.
New limestone lines streaked the grass.
                              Annie charged
towards the goal; in a year she'd be at Radcliffe,
later in Switzerland studying tree rings.
Past the halfback from Stevens School,
past their fullbacks, both teams
on her tail, she lifted the ball over to Megan
                              who flicked it in.
I jogged in the wings, my stick in my hands.
Their goalie tightened her knee pads;
everyone was hugging & jumping up & down;
I heard cheers from the stands; I had half the field
to myself & pictured Corky Miller, who, senior year,
led the team to a winning season,
her grown-up thighs pumping past the players.
She wore the plaid tunic of the varsity squad,
& when I met her on the stairs,
                              I had nothing to say.
I recall the smell of the oranges
the mothers served at half time,
the way we sat in a circle talking about the plays,
the stickiness of the lumpy wax we passed around
to preserve the wood on the snub-nosed sticks.
The light faded; we crowded into the cars,
exhausted, clutching our Latin books,
pressed against one another
in the cold November air.

POSING FOR THE PHOTOGRAPHER

At first I thought oh good what fun
like David Hemmings & Verushka
on the floor
but it wasn't
like that
against the wall
arranging my face
with you a mile away
across the room
waiting for the perfect 1/8 second.
Jesus what a job;
draped over the piano
was no good
my face among the plants
also lousy.
Let's talk this out
I wanted to say
like two adults.
Just tell me tell me
what to do.
No matter where I stand
or what I do
you get glare.

TRAINING THE DOG TO COME

is one of the hardest tasks your dog
will have to master. Start early.
Your dog will learn to sit & stay & heel;
perhaps he will read several elementary texts
before he's coming dependably. Do not be discouraged.
If it's summer & you've got one eye
on the raspberry bush, do not expect your dog to be fooled.
If it's fall & you're raking leaves,
your dog will be aware of this shift in your concentration,
& he'll probably take advantage
by taking a train into town.
Various methods may be employed at this juncture:
steak, leg of lamb, but we recommend
that you eliminate food as one incentive;
invest instead in several yards of parachute cord.
While your dog is browsing in the park,
cheerfully call *Come Boomer*
& reel him in. He should come trotting.
Off lead, you're competing with the carcasses of rabbits,
birds dead & alive, dogs just in from other cities
& a host of passionate instincts flickering
in & out of your dog's brain. He will not come.
He probably will not come for some time,
so you should be prepared for this.
In truth, your dog is not much interested in your affairs.
You will have to be more persuasive,
time your calling to coincide with his longing for you—
sporadic, at best, half-hearted.

ROSE'S POEM

If God will give you years, you have to prepare.
Dress like a lady; look like a lady; be a lady. I
used to be a walker. Now you see a statue that
puts on rouge & eyebrows & they say, *Rose, you
look beautiful.* If I get up in the morning, I say,
thank the good Lord. TV is a godsend, but no
one wants to know what's doing in the world.
They have their little groups. It's not for my
head to read newspapers; still, in a rich country
like America, I find poverty. Don't you see?
Someone's life is your story. I'm not much for
books, but I lived a life. As far as life goes, by
the time you get there, you lose your appetite
for going. To dance a hora in a circle ...
where does it get you? The same dance over
& over.

IV

DREAMING

for Leslie

We wake. You've been dreaming
of whales, of the way we incubate:
     ideas, preemies, birds, women,
anything needing time.

     I'm dreaming of Sausalito—
looking for a home or a harbor.
     This life without origin or resolution
rides like the rented car on borrowed cash.
     California's all low fog, sky,
and disappointing. But the whales!

     You've been watching their forelimbs
turning to flippers flashing
     in the soft green light
where a boy with blue-veined eyelids
     curls like a fern. Emerald. Sky.

     Night after night you return to the deep;
the baby floats in the liquid,
     and I speed south
on the San Bernardino Freeway
     heading for the mountains—
twelve lanes pointing to the pink horizon.

     I wake like someone sleeping at the wheel.
You rise like the nymph Callisto, who,
     transformed into a constellation,
became the Great Bear.

TOURISTS IN ITALY

for my parents

The rain has stopped and someone's mowing
the meadow behind the chicken coop.
All morning, I've been looking at pictures
of Italian hill towns. Outside, the laundry
hangs white and fresh on the line.
Earlier, I watched my friend
dip the chicken she had plucked
into a pot of boiling water. This made me proud.
I'm twenty-nine, my parents are alive,
and we have time to travel
to Postignano and Vitorchiano
where we'll walk up steep stairs
radiating from the church piazza.
There a boy in short pants sulks—
sweet face like my father's
in the photo taken when he was a boy at the fair.
Along the maze of slanting lanes,
I will pass with my mother and father
and we'll see fishing platforms—
lashed poles cantilevered from cliffs—
where women and men in blue pants
haul in lines
and take their catch
through the winding passageways
of Sperlonga.
Against the vernacular
architecture, my mother pauses
to watch the strong women
carrying mounds of dough.
In Pentadatillo, she stares from a promontory,
leaning on my father.
The rain-soaked stucco walls will drip,

we will admire the barns and castles,
laughing at the tiny stones trapped
inside our shoes, the burro heaped
with farm tools.

But here it's morning, Illinois,
the cabin where everything waits to be done:
the screened porch to be repaired,
jam jars filled with wildflowers.
This is not sad, nor is the sweeping
which must be done daily,
nor is the coming of evening in early July.
Outside the summer grass comes down,
the crystal throws a bar of color on the floor.
When I rise, I might be anyone
in a hill town, hurrying through an archway
into the populous summer streets.

THE ECHOLALIAC

The painter knows the moment when the canvas would speak.
   Sometimes I wake up dreaming
       on a word or phrase

       rocky jutting cove
       passageways   quonset

    She knew all the ramshackle places falling
    back to earth. I tagged along, she didn't
    mind. A few mangy goats brayed and the
    bare-footed kids played tag by the fence.
    She painted the trees and she painted the
    light looking back and forth from the
    paint to the painting.

        See this color? When you mix it, it becomes
        another shade of green.

        See this color?
            Another shade of green.

At five o'clock in the morning,
light pours through the summer trees.
Order is the most beautiful season.
I like to watch the young dogs
learning how to hunt. They seem surprised
by instinct, standing on the edge of the wood,
dying rabbits in their jaws.
The puppy tosses a chicken's head
into the air over and over. Late afternoon.
He plays in the garden, the bright head shines,
a blossoming zinnia.

I remember all the words I never said.
They form a blanket
that covers me at night.
Sometimes they rise from the table.
Someone boils water like tears,
sorry in the steam.

I am and am not another person in the room
where my words orbit theirs, the way
a refrain illuminates.

CAPTIVITIES

I want to tell you that you'll be all right,
but I don't know if you will be.

Long distance, tranquilized,
your words drift by like children
who lose interest in the game
and run home. You lost interest
for years at a time, returned to find
the world altered, familiar characters
relocated, no place to go.

Now I try to call you back with your name,
a word you recognized as you slipped from us.
Doctors. Friends. All sought the perfect formula.

2

I see you growing fat in your apartment.
Outside the light changes; you draw the shades.

At night do you feel hands and chests,
cavities opening and shutting
in the rhythm of your breath?
Do you touch yourself or
is your body a terrifying thing?

Our friends say you eat all day long
like the months between diet camp,
the slimming hostels where you threw
your body against walls and floors, bounced
with your heavyset comrades into town to binge.
Each August you returned—
thinner, tired, ready to start up again.
To eat or to starve, never to leave
the fortress of flesh.

3

I wished for you to marry
a nice man in business or a doctor,
someone like your father
who would take you off our hands.
In this, we failed you. We were your friends,
we believed you needed a custodian
for our fears.

Did I agree that you would never
earn your keep? That you would roam
around New York, cash the checks your family sent,
sit in cheap restaurants all winter?

Your voice drones; words run together
full of blame. And something in me rises,
wants to smack you into shape.
You're ruining the game; you quit
because you're behind
and there was a questionable call
and you never wanted to play anyway.

You're halfway down the street,
yelling, tears falling, and I
hug the dodgeball in my armpit,
scowl, tell the others to pick new teams,
wait for the grown-ups
to call us in.

SOMEONE ELSE'S CHILDREN

for Julia and Miriam Goodman

1

I wait all afternoon. Finally a child comes
banging up the stairs, yells *hello,* heads for
the fridge. She stands in front of the mirror
tugging on her corduroys. *They're too
short,* she whines.

2

From the apartment below, a flute recording.
Up here, piano practice.

3

A woman said, *I feel complete only when
I'm pregnant. I am not a biological parent,*
another woman said.

4

Neither am I. I borrow other people's
children to remind me of disasters I've dis-
carded: pants too short, lunch left behind,
best friends fighting, other people's rules.

SAILMAKER'S PALM

Low tide is full of rumors—
        brown bottles, wet gloves, wooden spoons—
fragments I gather & carry home
        to consider the hand:
the druggist's square & useful hand
        explains dosage & procedures,
is versatile, plays a violin all afternoon;
        the magician's hands wear the white, felt gloves
we wore as children, fool everybody once,
        get depressed & pile the cape & cane
beside the box where a third hand is quietly sawing.
        The cook's hand works in fits & starts,
loves action, strikes out for itself, never forgets
        an injury or a failure,
is moody by nightfall, basting & planning ahead.
        This brings us to yours—restless,
appreciative hands which do not aspire after holiness.
        When I take your hand, I feel it pull,
insistent on its own direction. Left alone,
        your hands pick on each other, siblings
struggling for dominion. I watch them argue at the table,
        disputatious to the end. I cannot grasp
the depth of their misunderstanding, the reasons why
        they suddenly fly to your face or tear into drawers.
In my dream, we're on a beach; you assemble the debris
        I collect—paint rag, table leg, bookshelf,
shirtsleeve—& we step back to admire your creation: a sailboat
        the size of an embrace. Before I can object,
you push it off—arms outstretched—& the jib fills.
        We stand for a long time watching
the boat, rugged as a sailmaker's palm—
        your hands dumb, satisfied.

CONFIGURATION

Like lists, our talks were pre-syntactical; each sequence,
like a fold of drapery, gave way, promised another varia-
tion. The conversation shimmered, prismatic, a Cézanne
landscape, whole fields left untouched.

This was the pleasure of the snowstorm: schedules im-
pounded; familiar streets undifferentiated; dogs poised
high on snowbanks. We passed invisible through solid
walls of snow, the narrow corridors blue with shadow.

When the first plow flashed and roared, cutting back the
drifts, when the block broke apart into *sidewalk, house,
street corner,* we exchanged old stories, perspective mov-
ing in like another act of God.

THE CONVERSION OF THE JEWS

I sat stiffly in the car, resisting
Sunday school & the public school kids
who swore & did it with boys. I went
to a private school during the week,
but in the Sunday school the kids didn't know
anything. Anything. Like when the teacher asked
what the Old Testament was,
I knew it was a source book,
a real history book, but they thought
it was all Jewish miracles.

Their fathers belonged to the Brotherhood
of the Temple & leaned on cars waiting for their kids
to come out with their foul mouths.
Their kids were smoking & touching in the bathroom,
& sometimes the girls peered over the stalls, snickering.
My father bought lox & bagels; it was Sunday &
the table was covered with cream cheese & stinking fish.

On Monday, I'd go to the other school, where
in Religion class, Christ was so handsome & young.
Sure, he had more color, more attraction
than those old guys who, though very smart,
were only making history.
We had Joseph with his coat of many colors
& his brothers & the beautiful Queen Esther.
I'd line up all our guys against theirs,
but somehow Christ, hanging pitiful from that cross—
the nails & spikes sticking into his head—
he always won.

I knew I was on the side of the Old Testament,
but the other kids on my side were so mean
I thought of going over to the New. And it's true
I got a little scared in Debbie Lawson's bedroom:
suspended above her bed, a wooden crucifix
with him hanging & a dime store photo of Mary.
There was no way out of religion

until in 6th grade, my friend Annie Post said
Religion was the Opiate of the People.
All those stories, she said—Christ & Moses & Buddha—
everybody had them. Afterwards we had new words
& unshakable beliefs: atheist, agnostic.
Afterwards I felt superior & knew they believed
because they needed to, because they couldn't stand knowing,
as Annie & I knew, that it was really accidents
in space, all chemistry & vapors.

FOR SARAH, HOME AFTER A WEEKEND
IN THE COUNTRY

I know how it feels; the fields are full of friends
and trees. A season
                    you never noticed like *that* before.
        You wake in a sleeping bag
                            in a barn, summer's
                    harvest spilling
                            onto the table,
                thick soup steaming.
Old dreams open like your eyes
which open like the pores of your body.
                            The dark mystery
                    of the evening
                resembles a feeling you cannot
                    name
                    but it feels like
                possibility.
And it does not leave you—
not next day or next week but lingers in your memory—
                    a square of wool, the color
                    of his shirt. You clear a space
            & the cat in your life curls up,
                reminds you of the safety,
        the   romance, the smell
of the apples that weekend
                        when friends were suddenly
        more than friends, trees *more* than trees,
your own self shuddering to fit
its sudden dimensions.

MORNING POEM

Listen. It's morning. Soon I'll see your hand reach
for my watch, the water will agitate in the kettle,
but listen. Traffic. I want your dreams first. And
to slide my leg beneath yours before the day opens.
Wait. We slept late. You'll be moody, the phone
will ring, someone wanting something. Let me put
my hands in your hair. Who I was last night I would
be again. This is how the future holds me, how de-
pression wakes with us; my body shelters it. Let me
put my head on your breast. I know nothing lasts.
I would try to hold you back, not out of meanness
but fear. Oh my practical, my worldly-wise. You
know how the body falters, falls in on itself. Tell me
that we will never want from each other what we
cannot have. Lie. It's morning.

POETRY FROM ALICE JAMES BOOKS

POETRY
ISBN 0-914086-36-7

$8.95

Wendy Gross

" 'Backtalk' presumes attending, and Robin Becker does—to family, friends, lovers, dogs, mountains, to memory. These poems, like the speaker in 'A Long Distance,' try to figure things out:

> *I remember the globe that was a pencil sharpener.*
> *I remember standing in the lunchroom*
> *& trying to figure out*
> *how I could be standing in the lunchroom*
> *& standing on the earth which was the globe.*

Standing on the earth, we engage in the common effort to say who we are, and to give that self our blessings. I admire Robin Becker's poems for the wit, tenacity, compassion they enlist in the labor."

—Carole Oles

"Robin Becker reminds me that to be a Jew or a feminist is to live with duality—of culture, language, and dream. The several warring parts of a complex identity—imposed, inherited, chosen—don't make easy sense. Events are funny, painful, awkward, unassimilable. With passionate intelligence, Becker conjures them for me, and I identify."

—Joan Larkin

alicejamesbooks

a writers' cooperative with an emphasis on publishing poetry by w
138 Mt. Auburn Street, Cambridge, Massachusetts 02138

ISBN 0-914086-36-7
9 780914 086369

SAMESEXMARRIAGEANDAMERICAN CONSTITUTIONALISM

A Study in Federalism, Separation of Powers, and Individual Rights

MURRAY DRY